Few plants or animals can survive in hot deserts

heat

Jennifer Fandel

A⁺

Smart Apple Media

COPYRIGHT

Published by Smart Apple Media

1980 Lookout Drive, North Mankato, MN 56003

Designed by Rita Marshall

Copyright © 2003 Smart Apple Media. International copyright reserved in all countries. No part of this book may be reproduced in any form without written permission from the publisher.

Printed in the United States of America

Photographs by JLM Visuals (John Minnich), Tom Myers, James P. Rowan, Tom Stack & Associates (J. Lotter, Bob Pool, Mark A. Stack, Ryan C. Taylor, Greg Vaughan, Dave Watts)

Library of Congress Cataloging-in-Publication Data

Fandel, Jennifer. Heat / by Jennifer Fandel. p. cm. – (Weather)

Includes bibliographical references and index.

Summary: Describes how the sun heats the earth, how buildings and pollution can increase Earth's temperature, and how important the right amount of heat is to keep the earth and its inhabitants functioning properly.

ISBN 1-58340-152-0

1. Heat budget (Geophysics)—Juvenile literature. 2. Heat—Physiological effect—Juvenile literature. [1. Heat.] I. Title. II. Weather (Smart Apple Media).

QC809.E6 F36 2002   551.5'253–dc21   2001049977

First Edition 9 8 7 6 5 4 3 2 1

Heat

CONTENTS

A Land Without Sun

Imagine a dark and cold place where nothing grows. The wind does not blow, clouds do not float across the sky, and no rain falls. This is what the earth would be like without the sun. The sun is the main ingredient in the earth's weather. The heat the sun gives off creates weather around the globe. The sun shines most directly on the middle of the earth, the equator, so it stays warm there year round. The North and South Poles receive only six months of sunlight. They lose

Antarctica is always cold because it gets little sunlight

more heat than they receive and stay cold all of the time. The earth tries to balance its **temperatures** by moving air around. This is how the sun's heat causes wind. The sun also causes rain: heat makes water **evaporate** and become clouds. When enough water collects in a cloud, it returns to the earth as rain (or snow if the air is cold).

How Heat Works

When the sun shines, light travels through the **atmosphere** to reach the earth. The clouds, water, and gases

Heat turns water into clouds, which then cause rain

Clouds and water absorb some sunlight and reflect some

of the atmosphere absorb a small amount of the sun's rays.

Most of the sunlight directly affects life on Earth. Land, water,

plants, and other objects absorb some of the sun's light, and

the rest is **radiated** to the atmosphere as

heat. This heat does not disappear

when the sun sets. The atmosphere works

like a blanket around the earth to keep heat

The hottest air temperature ever recorded on Earth was 136 °F (58 °C) in El Azizia, Libya, in 1922.

from escaping quickly. This is called the greenhouse effect. The

atmosphere is like the glass walls of a greenhouse. The glass

Like a greenhouse, Earth's atmosphere holds heat in

allows the sunlight to enter the greenhouse, where the plants

absorb some of the light. The rest of the light is reflected back

toward the greenhouse walls, which trap the heat inside.

The Amazing Atmosphere

Although the atmosphere acts like a blanket to keep the earth warm, it also keeps the earth from getting too hot.

The earth tries to keep its overall temperature at a steady 59 °F (15 °C) by losing the same amount of heat as it receives. Some scientists wonder if **The snow and ice on Antarctica reflect most of the sun's light, keeping the continent cold year round.** people are living in ways that harm the atmosphere and damage its ability to keep the earth from overheating.

> **Air pollution traps extra heat near the earth's surface**

Land, plants, and water absorb a lot of sunlight and use it to sustain life. While man-made structures absorb some of the sun's rays, they reflect much more back into the atmosphere as heat. As growing cities turn open land into highways and parking lots, more heat is added to the earth. More roads and buildings often

Leaves turn color in autumn because colder temperatures signal leaves to stop producing chlorophyll, which makes leaves green.

also mean cutting down trees, which absorb a lot of sunlight and radiate less heat. Pollution from factories and cars also causes problems because it traps heat close to the earth's

surface, raising temperatures in cities and towns where the

amount of pollution is high. Increased heat can harm certain

plants and animals and even affect the weather.

Cutting down too many trees might heat up the earth

A Careful Balance

Heat is essential for life to exist, but so is water. Imagine a farmer trying to grow food without either one!

Farmers need a balance of heat and water to keep their crops healthy. Without enough sun, plants may not sprout or grow properly. Without rain, high **When no rain falls and temperatures climb, farmers' fields often turn to dust. This is called a drought.** temperatures heat the land and strip the ground of its inner moisture. The soil cracks and turns to dust, and the crops shrivel and die. People and animals also need plenty of water

to balance the effects of high heat. If their bodies work too

hard in hot weather without receiving enough water, **heat**

exhaustion can occur. Heat is a necessary part of

We need a balance of heat and water to grow food

weather. It nourishes plants and animals, and causes wind and

rain. Since humans depend on the sun's heat to live, all people

must make sure that they take care of the earth and its

atmosphere. It is hard to imagine living **Crickets chirp more often when temperatures rise; you can esti-mate tempera-tures by listening to them.** in a world without any heat, or with too much heat. Maintaining just the right amount of heat requires a careful

balancing act by the earth and its atmosphere.

All life depends on receiving the right amount of heat

Observing Heat Differences

We know trees absorb more heat than most man-made structures. Land and water also absorb heat at different rates. See for yourself how heat affects each one.

What You Need

Two glass jars of equal size
Dirt or sand
Water
A thermometer (optional)

What You Do

1. Fill one jar with cool water.
2. Fill the other jar with cool sand or dirt.
3. Set both of the jars in a sunny place (outside or inside) for two hours.

What You See

When you put your finger (or the thermometer) into each jar, you will find that the dirt is warmer than the water. Dirt absorbs heat faster than water, but it also loses heat faster. If you placed the jars in a cool place for two hours, you would find that the dirt is cooler than the water.

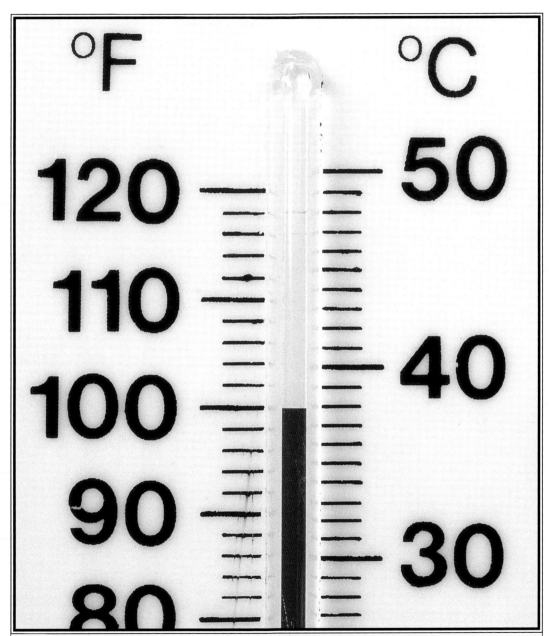

Heat may be measured on a Fahrenheit or Celsius scale

INFORMATION

Index

Words to Know

atmosphere (AT-mos-fear)—the protective layer of gases that surrounds the earth

evaporate (ee-VAP-uh-rate)—to change from a liquid to a gas

heat exhaustion (HEAT ig-zaws-chun)—a tired feeling from being exposed to too much heat, often without enough water

radiated (RAY-dee-ay-ted)—to spread or reflect the sun's rays

temperatures (TEM-per-a-cherz)—measurements of heat, usually in degrees Fahrenheit or degrees Celsius

Read More

Flanagan, Alice K. *Weather*. Minneapolis, Minn.: Compass Point Books, 2001.

Kerrod, Robin. *Weather*. Milwaukee, Wis.: Gareth Stevens Publishing, 1998.

Powell, Jillian. *Sun and Us*. Mankato, Minn.: Smart Apple Media, 1999.

Internet Sites

Kids' Weather Page from Penn State University
http://www.ems.psu.edu/WeatherWorld/kidstuff/meteor.html

The Weather Channel Information for Kids
http://www.weather.com/education/student/index.html

Play Time for Kids from the National Weather Service
http://www.nws.noaa.gov/om/reachout/kids.htm

The Weather Dude
http://www.wxdude.com